ICE MOUNTAIN

An Elegy

ICE MOUNTAIN

An Elegy

DAVE BONTA

ISBN 978-1-927496-12-1

Illustrations, design and editing
by Elizabeth Adams

First Edition

The collective work known as *Ice Mountain* is © Dave Bonta 2017.
Individual poems in *Ice Mountain* are published under a
Creative Commons Attribution-Share Alike 3.0 United States License

Published by Phoenicia Publishing, Montreal
www.phoeniciapublishing.com

For my parents

CONTENTS

Foreword 3
January 9
February 21
March 51
April 79
May 103
Notes 112
About the Author 115
About the Illustrations 117

Did We abolish Frost
The Summer would not cease -
If Seasons perish or prevail
Is optional with Us -

        Emily Dickinson

FOREWORD

This book owes its inception to a dog. For the first 17 days of 2014, I looked after an aging, half-blind Chesapeake Bay retriever named Canela, a sweet-tempered animal with her breed's typical winter-hardiness and extreme enthusiasm for, well, retrieving. We were outside by mid- to late-morning most days for a high-velocity exploration of the mountain where I've lived for the past 45 years, miles of urgent sniffing and listening punctuated by occasional, regrettable episodes of coprophagy. When we got back, Canela would flop down on her Dora the Explorer blanket and fall fast asleep, rumbling like an appliance with a bad motor.

She taught me a few new things. For example, having just circled the Far Field, more than anything Canela wanted to circle the Far Field: to paraphrase Heraclitus, it seems you can't circle the same field twice. During a brief thaw on January 14, she was exceptionally alert and alive to all the new smells, her head pivoting back and forth, while for me, everything had the same smell: wet dog. As Mary Oliver wrote, "A dog can never tell you what she knows from the smells of the world, but you know, watching her, that you know almost nothing." How well did I *really* know this mountain?

Canela missed her people dearly. They'd slipped away while we were on a walk, so trying to discover where they'd gone seemed to account for at least part of her drive to get out and scour the mountain at every opportunity, like a dervish searching for her lost Friend. When I handed her back, she leapt into the car without a backward glance and I returned to my slower-paced writer's life with a sigh of relief. The next day, two new inches of wind-blown snow covered all our tracks.

Two days later, I began the poetic journal that gave rise to this book. It turned out I missed those late-morning rambles with Canela, so I decided to see how much I could discover on my own, walking at a much slower pace but without the aid of a dog's nose to show me where a coyote had paused or which hollow logs might harbor rabbits or porcupines. The exploration continued when I sat down at the laptop, and I often ended up writing about things I'd remembered or thought about as I walked. I posted the drafts to my literary blog *Via Negativa* as a series of three-stanza poems of three lines each with the working title *Toward Noon*, looking ahead to the higher sun and longer days of spring.

The poetic form was inspired not by haiku but by the web comic *3eanuts*, which consists of old Peanuts cartoons stripped of the fourth, concluding panel, making them darker in tone but also more lyrical and open-ended. The intentional incompleteness of a "3verse" poem leads naturally to composition of another, and another... a good fit for a sequence of linked poems (or a single poem in 89 parts, if you prefer). The over-arching themes and connective tissue emerged organically and became clearer through revision. Some light fictionalization happened during the revision process: switching a few days here and there to make for smoother transitions, or replacing one observation with a different one from my pocket notebook. Otherwise it's straight nonfiction.

It might help if I provided a little geographic and ecological context. The Ice Mountain of the title is a high section of the Allegheny Front across the valley to the northwest of our own mountain (Brush Mountain, part of the westernmost ridge in the Valley and Ridge section of the Appalachians). In 2013 it was desecrated by an industrial wind plant, following an unsuccessful, six-year battle to stop it by a coalition of local and regional environmental groups. Why did we fight it so hard? The Allegheny Front is hugely important as a migration corridor for birds and bats as well as vital habitat for increasingly rare species such as the timber rattlesnake and the Allegheny woodrat, both of which are threatened by forest fragmentation. Two high-quality trout streams have also been impacted by the Ice Mountain wind plant. Wind turbines are especially deadly to golden eagles, which flow through here by the hundreds each November and March. Turbines also take a huge toll on forest bats—bats already imperiled by White Nose Syndrome.

Though held in public affection as symbols of green energy, poorly sited wind installations are no more benign than—say—hydroelectric projects, which were also promoted as a cleaner alternative to burning coal back in the day, before their toll on wildlife and interruption of core ecological functions could no longer be ignored. The mild form of mountaintop removal that occurs when industrial wind plants are installed on Appalachian ridgetops is of course nowhere near as horrific as the destruction that coal mining entails, and to the extent that wind power might replace some small fraction of coal power, it could even be seen as a good thing. But in reality, the Appalachians don't have high-quality wind resources—not compared to coastal and offshore sites, for example—simply far fewer wealthy and powerful people to mount NIMBY campaigns.

So once again the Appalachians are a national sacrifice area. The turbines on Ice Mountain and elsewhere in the region are the latest example of a continuous series of boom-and-bust economic cycles based on ecologically catastrophic resource extraction. Here in central Pennsylvania, east of the Front, we're spared the direct ravages of coal mining, so it could be worse. But these mountains were badly clear-cut for the charcoal iron industry in the first half of the 19th century, which let to massive erosion of slow-growing forest soils. In the latter half of the 19th and first decades of the 20th century, the remaining forests of the east were clear-cut during the timber boom, creating what newspapers at the time called the Great Pennsylvania Desert. Much of the region is thought to have become permanently warmer at that time due to the widespread eradication of eastern hemlock stands on north- and west-facing slopes, replaced by oaks and other deciduous species. Our soils have been further damaged by acid deposition in rain, fog and snow, thanks to the coal-burning power plants to our west. (A part of me winces every time we get more snow, knowing that it's laden with all kinds of nasty pollutants—more so than rain.) In recent years, hydrofracking for methane, heavily promoted by Pennsylvania politicians from both parties, has continued the state's economic addiction to the exploitation of nature.

As a poet, I have a hard time even discussing these things without succumbing to the deadening chill of words like "environment" and "resources"—plastic words, as the German thinker Uwe Poerksen calls them, designed to obscure and distance rather than to clarify. But another, more vital jargon does animate a few of the poems in *Ice Mountain*: the language of geology, which has delighted me since I was a kid. Thanks to my geographer brother Mark, I've recently come to appreciate the impact of periglacial processes on the modern landscape of central Pennsylvania, which was south of the furthest extension of the continental ice sheets but still close enough for permafrost conditions and various exotic processes related to that.

Globally speaking, we are still in the tail end of the glacial period. The winter of 2014 was in many ways like the ones I remember from my childhood in the 1970s: long, cold, snowy, and giving way to spring with exquisite slowness, every day like a new revelation. With predictions of climate change growing all the time more dire, I don't know how many more winters like it I'll get to see.

Dave Bonta
Plummer's Hollow, Pennsylvania
September 2016

JANUARY

22 January 2014

in the owl's flight
as in the conifers it left
that late-morning silence

and at the woods' edge
the frozen carcass of a cow
pecked at by chickadees

bare trees like forks
the sky too is a dish
best served cold

23 January

looking at bird tracks in the snow
I feel a certain anxiety
of influence

and just one phone line
for all the caravans of the internet
its wavy shadow

I chew on a piece of congealed
black cherry sap
from a head-sized burl

25 January

a nuthatch is at the window
probing under the sill
for edible flotsam

through the reflected branches
perhaps it sees a pale face
swim up behind the glass

that odd ice
impossible to taste
with its year-round winter

26 January

the old-timers knew better
than to build right on top of a ridge
so I have to climb for the view

off to the northwest
Ice Mountain looms
so much higher than here

pinned down with turbines
like a felled mammoth
the spears still quivering

27 January

in the oak's crown
the sound of porcupine teeth
a dry scraping

ahead of me on the path
the tracks of three deer
braid and unbraid

something scratches my chest
I reach into my coat and pull out
a claw-shaped twig

28 January

high gusts of wind
my footprints in the snow
are raised up and scattered

I press an ear to the trunk
of a ridge-top oak
nothing but creaking

a woodpecker must hear
any sound a tree can make
it taps out a response

29 January

five below zero
the stream banks are thick with dirt-
capped columns of needle ice

minor relicts of the glacial epoch
when cryogenic perturbation
rearranged the ground

cliffs crumbled hillsides slumped
the super-stability we know now
a gift of frost and thaw

30 January

on a low mound in the woods
two coyotes have left
overlapping turds

like graffiti tags made
of hair and small bones
I follow their tracks

until they diverge in an old clearcut
choked with the alien invasive
tree-of-heaven

31 January

all this time
six well-used deer beds
were just out of sight from the porch

trees' skinny shadows
bending with the contours of the snow
what else have I failed to notice

the old outhouse
half-fallen into its hole
how long has the roof been gone

FEBRUARY

1 February

the dark ridges
to the east are edged
with yellow light

overhead the same dull
white as the ground
I pull the shades for a nap

a low thumping
where a groundhog stirs
under the floor

2 February

at first I mistake
their distant yelps for coyotes
so unusual is the sound of children outdoors

after a good tracking snow
my brothers and I were always keen
to play Fox and Hounds

I was the best fox
I would circle back find a likely tree
and take cover in the sky

3 February

vole tunnels are dimly visible
blue as varicose veins
in the thinning snow

as I take my coffee grounds
each day neatly wrapped
in its filter-shroud

out to the compost pit
to join the bright frozen rinds
of tropical fruit

4 February

In a dream I run
through my half-remembered high school
still an outcast

I grew up with a woodstove
instead of a television
I know all the theme songs of oak

the crackle and bang
the hiss and whistle and sudden
sigh of collapse

5 February

I remember the chicken-
killing dog
my brother's pet

and the gray fox that sat
and gazed at us like an angel
one that foamed at the mouth

holding a rifle
is like holding an infant
wary of setting it off

6 February

our neighbor plows
down-hollow and back
his wife riding shotgun

the old plow truck hasn't left
the mountain in years
bound to its one road

in each yard
it raises white ramparts
from the fallen enemy

7 February

fresh holes gape in a maple
where a pileated woodpecker has extracted
sleeping grubs

I keep breaking through
the new smooth ground of ice and sleet
it hasn't quite set

on the plowed road the male
and female cardinal are gathering
stones for their gizzards

8 February

opossum out at mid-day
on the glare ice
wipes its snout with its paws

it's digging through the crust
to reach food we've pitched
old barbecue sauce rotten cabbage

inserting its head
as if through the shell
of a great white egg

9 February

a bark ode in response to Gary Barwin

it's only in strong sun
that the winter woods resemble
a bar-coded label

today is gray
I pause to stroke the bark
of a diseased chestnut oak

ridges kinked and folded
ordinarily straight lines
impossible to read

10 February

the slow and steady
accumulation of snow
making everything strange

reminds me of my dad
reading aloud to the family
from a book in his lap

the whisper of pages turning
each of us building a picture
all our own

11 February

the crest of Ice Mountain
once harbored a rare scrub barrens
ancient trees made wayward by the wind

as I start up the ridge my tired knees
make quiet popping noises
with every step

Sancho I say to myself
those windmills aren't giants
they're flowers for the dead

12 February

the squirrel's tracks end
in a smudge of blood on the snow
one tuft of fur

and the long furrow
its dangling tail drew
beside the fox's footprints

in the field a bulldozer
lowers its blade
to a white and heavy harvest

13 February

the spruce grove
at the top of the hollow
harbors a north-woods chill

seated on a runner sled
I hurtle down
into the sunlit field

my shadow like a witching rod
stretched out before me
alive to every swell and swale

14 February

it snowed all night
I dreamt an opossum slept between us
with its death-head grin

by first light
the old dog statue in the yard
is buried up to its neck

let's get a bowl of fresh snow
not to eat but just to admire
like cut flowers

15 February

a cottontail has squeezed
through a ring of fencing
to browse on dogwood sprouts

the snow squeaks under my boots
as I loom up
and it forgets how to escape

the small animal
beating against its cage
like a panicked heart

16 February

breaking trail with snowshoes
I choose to believe I'm half-floating
not half-sinking

here's a sudden mine shaft
where a squirrel found
the precise spot it buried a nut

clumps of snow sail off the trees
making a random scatter
of oblong tracks

17 February

the house is engulfed
by heavy snow
glassy tentacles stretch toward the ground

relentless accuracy
is the nature of this octopus
gathering strength with each new storm

my head fills with mucus
let me too be replenished
in nightly increments

(lines in italics from Marianne Moore, "An Octopus")

18 February

house-bound by a cold
I research last winter's installation
of the 25 turbines on Ice Mountain

workers *battled subzero temperatures*
high winds hilly terrain and large
amounts of snow

in crawler cranes said to balance
brute strength and ease of mobility
to deliver a compact footprint

(lines in italics from manitowaccranes.com)

19 February

having melted
the snow above it
a black stone glistens in its pit

all thaws seem abrupt
lichens slicked with meltwater
glow a lurid green

I'm feverish
might I too burn a hole
clear through to spring

20 February

a few degrees above freezing
and already the first gnats
have reanimated

insects have mastered
the most immaculate lifelessness
deader than any corpse

cells so flooded with glycerin
even ice with its many knives
never gets to grow

21 February

the melting snowpack
uncovers old scandals
two spots of blood a clump of feathers

here are the twigs and dead leaves
scattered by high winds
just after New Year's

it's like a palimpsest in reverse
the later texts erased
one by one

22 February

trees sway drunkenly
in a sudden gust of wind
the clacking of their branches

the whole hillside
is in motion around me
standing here

with my cold almost gone
how marvelous it is
just to breathe

23 February

in a snow-bound ring of stones
I am burning all the tissues
from my cold

the sun beats down
fallen twigs are melting themselves
into form-fitting graves

a flat wing of ash
floats up
and hangs in the air

24 February

clouds pull their shadows
across the snow-filled valley
as if dragging for a drowned swimmer

I watch from the ridge
mesmerized by the alternation
of gloom and glare

the *no hunting* sign rattles
on the electric pole
above the deep claw-marks of bears

26 February

the foundation of the fallen-in house
now seems hardly big enough
for a closet

let alone three floors
of moldering furniture
and typewriters full of dead beetles

up in the woods a beech tree
has erased the vacant spot beside it
with outstretched limbs

27 February

when it died the porcupine
leaked its fluids onto the snow
like a junker car

I turn it over
with a long stick
no sign of a wound

startled up from the forest floor
sixteen doves go whistling
into the snow squall

28 February

the sky lacks
the thinnest
whisker of cloud

jets untethered by contrails
hardly seem to roar
lost in all that blue

this was the sky I labored at
with crayons at age five
having given up on the sun

MARCH

2 March

day by day the shadows shrink
grow fatter
stay closer to home

adjusting their ambitions
to a more realistic assessment
of the horizon

but before the ice age
even these mountains
were precipitous

3 March

I was land-hungry
in my younger days
I turned the soil each summer

and in winter hoped for snow
a Platonic kind of field
as empty as a desert

what good was all that yearning
and the leafless rose
with its tangle of barbed canes

4 March

Ice Mountain's propellers
spin at different speeds
face this way and that

you can't hear them from here
their low-frequency moans
like lost whales

what won't we sacrifice
to keep the weather just right
inside our homes

5 March

small birds fly up
into the bare branches
of the walnut trees

the phone rings
someone we know has had
another breakdown

at the sound of my voice
six deer delicate as ballerinas
raise their tails to leap

6 March

a cop with a backpack sprayer
poisoning an urban garden
why should I dream of this

I carry out a dead houseplant
but can't find a snow-free spot
to lay it down

the house finch whose eye disease
prevents him from migrating
warbles on and on

7 March

paper birch trees can only bend
so far before they break
under the weight of freezing rain

rhododendron leaves
tough as old scrolls are stripped
by starving deer

but some always resprout from the roots
having who knows how many
lifetimes of practice

8 March

slush is the mellifluous sound
the tires make just before
they start spinning

soft snow banks
are treacherous as Loreleis
pulling the unwary driver in

I steer gingerly with windows down
listening to the welcome hiss
of leaves and mud

9 March

each time I go out
I interrupt something
a hawk's meal a groundhog's courtship

I make an offering of my gray hair
toss the cuttings out
onto the snow

the warm wind
like an awkward guest
carries them back in

10 March

the naked ground seems
at first an oversight
then a spreading crisis

the brown earth without any papers
poor beyond belief
is taking over

snow retreats to the woods
shrinking into islands of foolscap
between the trees

11 March

a groundhog comes out of her hole
and begins to gather
bundles of dried grass

harlequin ladybird beetles
emerge from cracks and crannies
in the side of the house

land on a patch of snow
to quench their thirst
and stumble to a frozen halt

12 March

snow has gone
from the big rockslide
just below the crest of the ridge

what geologists call a block slope
the ice-felled ruins
of a former summit

I hop from boulder to boulder
arms out for balance on those
that still shift

13 March

in memoriam Bill Knott

news of your death
came as a cold front brought
a skim of snow

it vanishes at the sun's touch
soon only the trees' shadows
are still white

like the bones of some Pleistocene beast
undone by any lapse
of glacial chill

14 March

no vision can equal
the sharp-edged clarity of winter
especially in retrospect

on a warm day a patch of ice
dulls over
like a dead eye

inhabited by empty rooms
that split and join
as meltwater bubbles through

15 March

the highway's tar has been bleached
by a winter's worth of salt
and in the mid-day sun

it almost shines
I squint at the shapes on the shoulder
as I pass

here some saltaholic's crumpled fur
there a fetal curl
of flayed tire

17 March

a gray day in March
is the best time to go hunting
for teaberries

sharp and sweet
after all those months
of frozen burial

bright as fresh drops of blood
under the glossy wings
of wintergreen

19 March

the pale red-tailed hawk
harried by crows
glides along the ridge

and lands in a stand
of black locusts broken
by last December's ice storm

one more pale wound
among the ragged spears
of raw wood

20 March

the outermost spruce trees
rock in the wind
a grouse feather floats down

there's an owl pellet
in the middle of the trail
a gray gris-gris of rodent bones

I enter the grove
careful as a bridegroom
at each raised threshold of root

22 March

the first phoebe of spring
hovers in front of me
drawn by a slow fly

in my email a scan
of a tintype portrait
I sat for last August

eyes of silver nitrate
squinting without my glasses
waiting to blink

23 March

earth tones is a term
no recent migrant from the tropics
would understand

how a dormant earth
can come in moss-green
bark-gray and a thousand browns

umber ochre
sienna
burnt or otherwise

24 March

on a maple sapling's bark
a zigzag ladder
maybe the old tooth-marks of a snail

green continents of moss
beckon across a fluttering
sea of brown leaves

*this cloud-filtered sunlight
is perfect* says the photographer
as her cheeks slowly turn red

26 March

after a hundred years of reaching
for the same small
portion of filtered sunlight

these three witch hazel trunks
have begun to merge
the ground bulges over their common roots

back home you hold a tape
along your outstretched arms
measuring for knitwear

27 March

most of the goldenrods still standing
at winter's end are topped by
the empty nurseries of wasps

dried half-pods of milkweed
cluster three to a stalk
a baroque superfluity of arch and wing

the low accelerating throb
of a drumming grouse
reminds me what real wings can do

28 March

petrichor that musk
the soil gives off after rain
is strongest when long delayed

we breathe deeply
watching two male pileated woodpeckers
hitch their way down a tree

side by side cackling softly
dividing it
between them

30 March

the March winds have blown
wet snow sideways
against the trees

look in one direction
and the woods are white
in the other brown

the snow sticks to our boot soles
lifting like lids
from jars of earth

APRIL

1 April

small murky ponds
appear in late winter
at the top of the watershed

now dozens of wood frogs
having just reanimated
from their cryogenic sleep

float through the reflected treetops
lust blatting
from each fat throat

2 April

below the stone well
the garter snakes thread themselves
into a love knot

but there's no female
just a male releasing female pheromones
and they soon untangle

and circle restlessly like eddies of wind
old skins whispering
through dead grass

4 April

the field sparrow is back
that rising trill spilling
from a small pink beak

a yellow-bellied sapsucker taps
a ring of wells
all around the bole of a hickory

bundled in British wool
you sunbathe on the porch
listening to the polyglot creek

6 April

camera at the ready
you stalk a mourning cloak
avid as a book thief

for that two-page
spread of darkness
glowing in the leafless woods

you and the butterfly
equally alert
to the vicissitudes of light

8 April

a winter wren darts low
over the rushing stream
and unwinds its hurdy-gurdy song

not all water-lovers
are bouyant in the same way
the waterthrush walks on the bottom

tail bobbing
as if spring-loaded
while we stand dripping in the rain

9 April

on Ice Mountain
the bone-clean blades
are scything the air

how many crumpled wings
might be scattered
among the old stumps

we can't walk there now
someone might get hurt
they say

10 April

just after your departure
I find half a hummingbird nest
and an old broken crock

the sun comes out
a fly circles the lip
of a purple crocus

the kestrel hunting meadow voles
keeps returning to the same
spot on the wire

11 April

the phoebes across the road
carry beakfuls of mud
into their nest

I'm planting onions with my hands
fingernails harvesting
dark crescents

this summer while I'm gone
the walking onions will re-plant themselves
head-down in the dirt

13 April

on the first warm day
the mountain hums with insects
and the valley with motorcycles

between twists of old coyote scat
and dried grass curled
tight as pubic hair

flat against the ground
the trailing arbutus's
fragrant parts ease open

15 April

what would the wind do without
the daffodils' yellow
hoopla of blooms

tree leaves are still packed
tight as gunpowder
in their slim cartridges

when the wind brings
the rumor of a storm
only the rhododendron turns pale

17 April

the sun slips over
the gray pelt of a vole zipping
from one hole to another

and catches on a distant gleam
of frost-heaved glass
luring me to go look

an antique beer bottle
bluer than a blue baby
rests in a cradle of leaves

19 April

an oak tree toppled in a high wind
20 years ago has rotted
almost to nothing

leaving just the twist of roots
spokes of a rimless wheel
a crippled star

as if whatever hardness
kept it from holding tight
now won't let it go

20 April

a chickadee in the garden
fills its beak with thistle down
and flies off to its nest

I take a closer look
that wasn't down but my own hair
from last month's haircut

a spring azure butterfly
lands on the bluestone road
folds its wings and vanishes

21 April

the soft notes of
a blue-headed vireo
draw me away from my desk

I smell manure from the valley
as I watch the vireo
snatching insects from the air

night's dust on my glasses
becomes a veil of gauze
in the noon-time sun

22 April

the sun comes out
in the middle of a shower
too high for a rainbow

unless you imagine
the bird's-eye view
rainbow against the ground

and off to the side in avian vision
the radiant shimmer
of this magnet Earth

24 April

still cold at 11:30
and the hepaticas are only half-open
nodding on their thin stalks

my mother tallies them
with stroke-marks
in her pocket notebook

at the top of a hemlock tree
a porcupine sleeps
in a sunlit halo of quills

25 April

mayapples are coming up
green parasols shedding soil
as they open

a coyote trots
across the road
glancing at me over its shoulder

above the trembling surface
of a vernal pond
the first warblers' buzzy songs

26 April

I eat my enemies by the handful
spicy leaves of the invasive
garlic mustard

back at home I strip
in front of the mirror
checking for bloodthirsty ticks

a squirrel walks past the window
with bulging cheeks
carrying one of her young

28 April

the shadbush is in bloom
a small cloud on the cliff
above the railroad tracks

as I drive up the hollow
on our one-lane road
a red-tailed hawk passes me going down

all the spring ephemerals are emerging
leaves wrinkled and damp
like freshly pitched tents

29 April

low clouds hide the turbines
on Ice Mountain
and it looks like a mountain again

down below there's the ugly subdivision
where a black family once woke
to a burning cross

I find a shed antler on the powerline
a twisted Y
like the bottom half of a stick figure

30 April

after all-night rain
the forest floor is soft
and full of give

a birch log crumbles when I step on it
but the bark arches back
as I raise my foot

new ferns uncoil
heads slowly dissolving
into spine and ribs

MAY

1 May

searching for morels
I find only
a gutted puffball

I nudge the intact part
with the point of my umbrella
it's all out of smoke

ovenbird nests and the black morel
writes a friend
impossible to see

2 May

a haze of jewelweed sprouts
the dimpled embryonic leaves
like conjoined twins

from the valley the sound
of an Amish buggy
horseshoes clattering on the road

a crooked sassafras beside the trail
something has found under its bark
a blood-colored door

3 May

is that gobbling on the ridge
a turkey or a turkey hunter
that whistle is it a train or the paper mill

I follow a vole's progress
by watching where the grass trembles
until a breeze springs up

how the weasel must hate the wind
how it must strive to sound
exactly like it

5 May

the first surveyor in 1795
labeled this mountain *Violet Hill*
did he study it in the blue distance

or see right at his feet
the crowds of violets fluttering
under the attention of the rain

a warbler just back from the tropics
sings quietly
as if trying to locate all the notes

6 May

the beech tree has seven eyes
where limbs used to be
each of them gazing upward

away from the scars of old knife-cut graffiti
smoke up fly high
Manson lives

a black-throated green warbler
forages in a neighboring oak
its shadow crossing my face

7 May

it's like telling a rosary
this counting of warblers
worm-eating hooded cerulean black-throated blue

and later
when a black rat snake rears up
like an instant tree

I remember all the deadly false Edens
the birds fly into
those acres of glass

10 May

goldfinches gad about
in the blossoming crowns of the oaks
brassy as advertising

the clouds draw in
wood thrushes begin
their evening songs at noon

long feathers of rain on the breeze
a plumage the exact
color of the world

NOTES

22 January
"the frozen carcass of a cow": Deliberately placed for a camera-trap, part of a program to track the movements of golden eagles in the Appalachians (and also document the presence of other cool animals, such as fishers and bobcats).

29 January
"cryogenic perturbation": A fancy way to say "frost heaving."

6 February
Our neighbors are Troy and Paula Scott. There are three houses in Plummer's Hollow altogether: mine, the Scotts', and my parents'.

9 February
"in response to Gary Barwin": The experimental Canadian poet, an online acquaintance, has a special fascination with the aesthetic qualities of barcodes.

11 February
"a rare scrub barrens": That was the conclusion of Western Pennsylvania Conservancy biologists who evaluated the site (Thomas Saunders, personal communication).

18 February
The quotes are from a press release, "Manitowoc crawlers confront frosty conditions on Ice Mountain" (6/25/2013), and a product description page for the Model 18000 lattice boom crawler.

24 February
"*no hunting* sign": In point of fact, the property is posted for hunting by written permission only.

2 March
"these mountains were precipitous": Farther south in West Virginia, where periglacial effects would've been less intense, the first ridge east of the Allegheny Front still sports a rocky Mohawk in some places (most famously at Seneca Rocks), and the ridges lack extensive toeslopes of colluvium (the poorly sorted rubble that flows downslope under periglacial conditions).

6 March
"eye disease": "Mycoplasmal conjunctivitis, as the disease is commonly called, is caused by a unique strain of *Mycoplasma gallisepticum*, a parasitic bacterium previously known to infect only poultry." —Project FeederWatch feederwatch.org/learn/house-finch-eye-disease/

1 April
"small murky ponds": The reference is to what ecologists variously refer to as vernal ponds, ephemeral ponds/pools, or seasonal pools. They're of ecological significance precisely because of their ephemerality, which makes them unsuitable for fish and therefore ideal as nurseries for wood frogs and several species of salamanders.

2 April
"a male releasing female pheromones": Apparently a common behavior among eastern garter snakes, which biologists attribute to a desire to get warm. (This is also the time when most actual mating takes place—just after emergence, as with wood frogs.)

22 April
"avian vision": "The magnetic field or magnetic direction may be perceived as a dark or light spot which lies upon the normal visual field of the bird." —Biologist Dominik Heyers, quoted in "Birds Can 'See' Earth's Magnetic Field," *National Geographic News*, September 27, 2007.

7 May
"all the deadly false Edens the birds fly into": "Up to a billion birds die in collisions with glass each year in the United States. ... Both common and rare bird species hit windows. According to a 2014 study, species commonly reported in glass collisions include White-throated Sparrow and Dark-eyed Junco. Ruby-throated Hummingbirds are frequent victims, along with Wood Thrush and other species of conservation concern."
—American Bird Conservancy, abcbirds.org/program/glass-collisions/

ABOUT THE AUTHOR

Dave Bonta is a writer, editor, and web publisher. He's perhaps most widely known as the publisher of *Moving Poems*, a daily compendium of poetry videos from around the web. His own videopoems have been screened in galleries and festivals in Buenos Aires, Athens, and Leicester, U.K. In 2010, Phoenicia Publishing brought out *Odes to Tools*, a small book of 25 poems that originally appeared at his literary blog *Via Negativa*. Another Via Negativa-derived collection, *Breakdown: Banjo Poems*, was selected by Sascha Feinstein as co-winner of the 2011 Keystone Chapbook Prize and published by Seven Kitchens Press. *Ice Mountain* is his first full-length print collection.

Dave lives on a mountaintop in central Pennsylvania as well as on the internet. He serves on the board of the Juniata Valley Audubon Society, based in Altoona, PA., despite the fact that he says he's "not a real birdwatcher."

ABOUT THE ILLUSTRATIONS

Beth Adams is a graphic designer, writer, artist, and the founder of Phoenicia Publishing. She grew up in the woods and fields of central New York State, and her first job, long before moving to Vermont and later, Montreal, was as a naturalist, artist and exhibit designer for the New York State Department of Environmental Education. She now maintains a studio in Montreal, where she has lived since 2008. From 2005 to 2013, she served with Dave Bonta as co-managing editor and advisory editor for the online literary magazine, *qarrtsiluni*.

The illustrations created for this book are linocut relief prints, hand-printed on Japanese paper, and most are available as limited edition prints, also benefitting local and regional conservation efforts in central Pennsylvania.

Credits: The cover illustration is based on a photograph by Rachel Rawlins. The Owl is based on a photograph by Richard Walker, and the Eastern Cottontail on a photograph by Marit & Toomas Hinnosaar, both licensed under Creative Commons copyright. Other images are based on photographs by the illustrator, the author, or attribution-free images from Wikimedia.

A NOTE ON THE TYPE

The interior text typeface is Adobe Garamond Pro, designed by Robert Slimbach in 1989 as an interpretation of original roman and italic faces by the French type designers Claude Garamond (1505-1561) and Robert Granjon (1530-1590). The display type used in the headlines is Lithos, designed in 1989 by Carol Twombly for Adobe Systems, and inspired by ancient Greek architectural inscriptions.

ABOUT PHOENICIA PUBLISHING

Phoenicia Publishing is an independent press based in Montreal but involved, through a network of online connections, with writers and artists all over the world. We are interested in words and images that illuminate culture, spirit, and the human experience. A particular focus is on writing and art about travel between cultures—whether literally, through lives of refugees, immigrants, and travelers, or more metaphorically and philosophically—with the goal of enlarging our understanding of one another through universal and particular experiences of change, displacement, disconnection, assimilation, sorrow, gratitude, longing and hope.

We are committed to the innovative use of the web and digital technology in all aspects of publishing and distribution, and to making high-quality works available that might not be viable for larger publishers. We work closely with our authors, and are pleased to be able to offer them a greater share of royalties than is normally possible.

Your support of this endeavor is greatly appreciated.

Our complete catalogue is online at www.phoeniciapublishing.com

www.ingramcontent.com/pod-product-compliance
Lightning Source LLC
LaVergne TN
LVHW020934090426
835512LV00020B/3357